A SIMPLE EXPLORATION
OF THE UNIVERSE,
EVOLUTION, AND PHYSICS

WHERE
Did We
COME FROM?

#1 BESTSELLING
SCIENCE AUTHOR FOR KIDS
CHRIS FERRIE

Sourcebooks
eXplore

FIRST THE QUARK

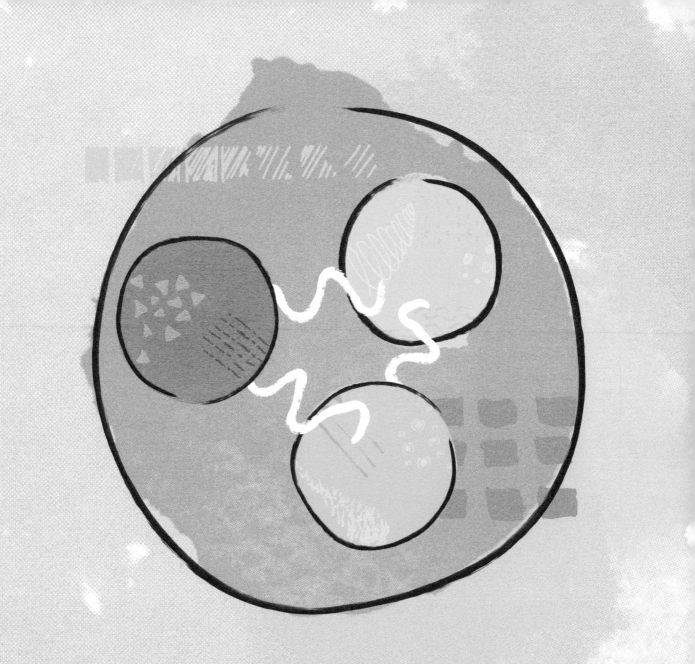

THEN THE PARTICLE

FIRST THE ATOM

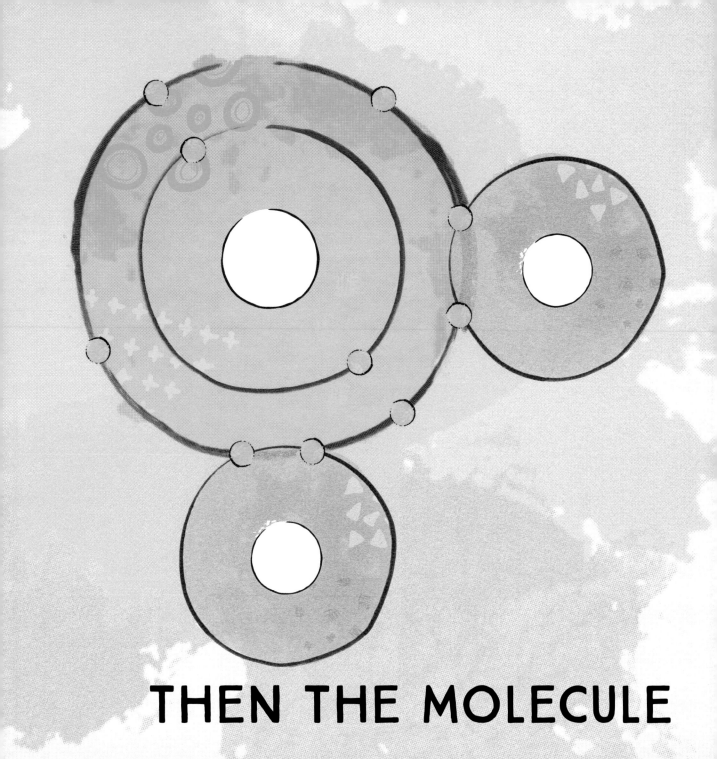

THEN THE MOLECULE

FIRST THE SUN

THEN THE SOLAR SYSTEM

FIRST THE EARTH

THEN THE LIFE

FIRST THE GENE

THEN THE MUTATION

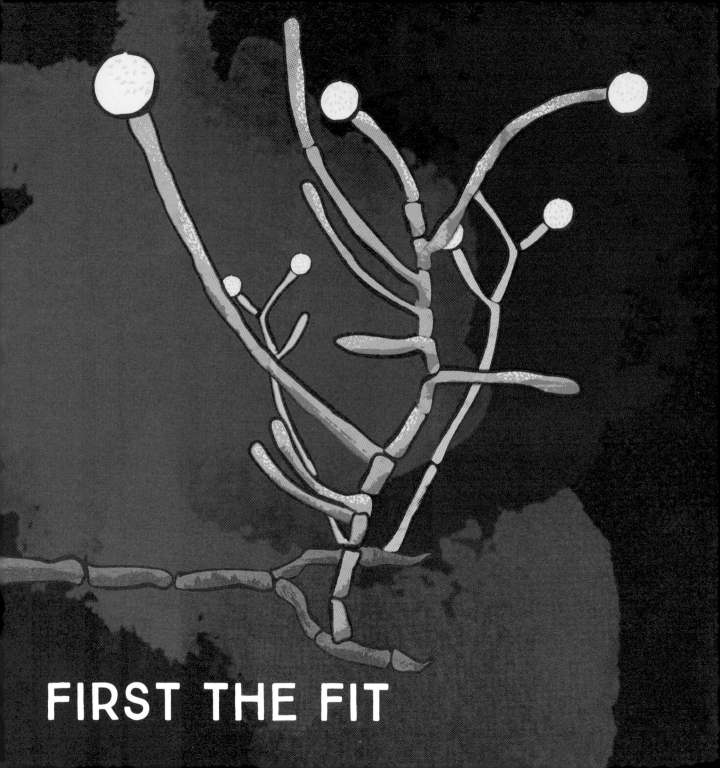

FIRST THE FIT

THEN THE FITTEST

FIRST THE TRIBE

THEN THE CIVILIZATION

FIRST THE LOVE

THEN THE CHILD

FIRST THE SCHOOL

THEN THE DEGREE

FIRST THE PRACTICE

THEN THE EXPERTISE

FIRST THE SCIENTIST

FIRST THE HYPOTHESIS

THEN THE EXPERIMENT

FIRST THE EXPERIMENT

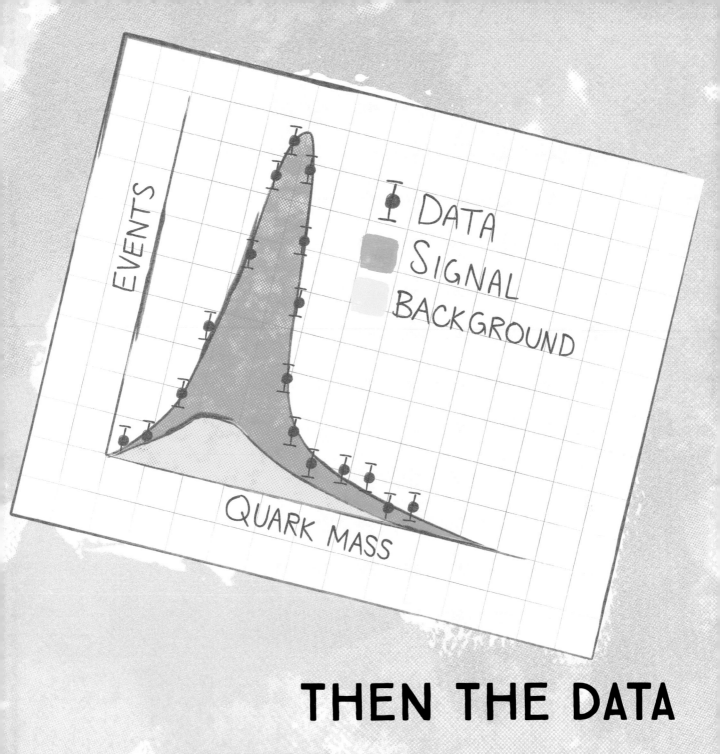

THEN THE DATA

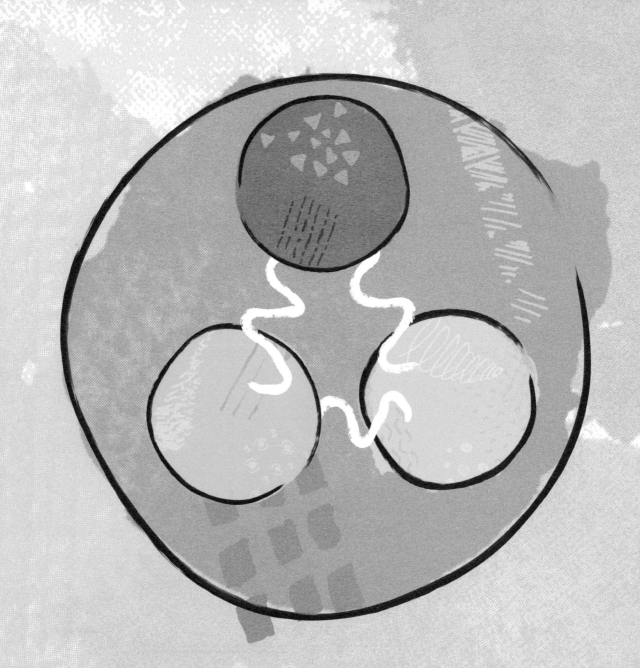

FIRST THE PARTICLE

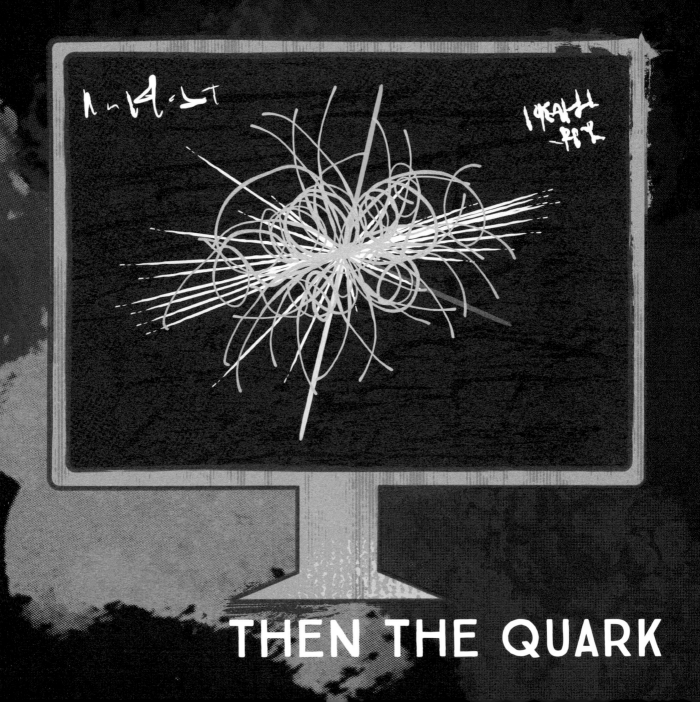

THEN THE QUARK

FIRST THE QUARK. Pictured: a model of a quark as a simple ball. Quark (rhymes with **fork**) is the name given to six of twelve elementary particles of matter. The six types have funny names like up, down, top, bottom, strange, and charm! Quarks are too small to see, so they are drawn as little balls.

THEN THE PARTICLE. Pictured: a model of a proton with the strong force represented as wiggling lines. Quarks combine to make larger particles. Three quarks create a proton or neutron. These are held together with the strong force—one of four fundamental forces of nature.

FIRST THE ATOM. Pictured: the "planetary model" of hydrogen with the nucleus at the center and an electron orbiting around it. An atom is made of protons, neutrons, and electrons. The core is called the nucleus and is packed with protons and neutrons. Electrons move around the nucleus. Each atom is one of a type called an element. The simplest element is hydrogen.

THEN THE MOLECULE. Pictured: a model of an H_2O molecule and its two bonds, which have the hydrogen and oxygen share electrons. Atoms combine to make molecules. Most everything you see around you is made of molecules. The most important molecule to you is H_2O—water—which is made of one oxygen atom and two hydrogen atoms.

FIRST THE SUN. Pictured: a typical depiction of the Sun and its corona (its outermost atmosphere). The Sun is one of thousands of stars we can see with our naked eyes (but never look at it directly!), and one of billions upon trillions in our universe. The Sun is mostly hydrogen pulled together by gravity. It burns hydrogen like fuel, making other elements and giving warmth to the Earth.

THEN THE SOLAR SYSTEM. Pictured: the Sun and eight planets, excluding poor Pluto, which is no longer categorized as a planet. The solar system includes all the objects—like planets, moons, asteroids, and comets—that orbit the Sun. The eight planets are Mercury, Venus, Earth, Mars, Jupiter, Saturn, Uranus, and Neptune. But there are over a million known objects in our solar system.

FIRST THE EARTH. **Pictured: Earth seen from space with its blue oceans and green land covered by white clouds in a thin atmosphere.** Earth is the planet we live on. It is the only known place in the universe that is home to life. The Earth is large but the atmosphere and oceans, which support life, are very thin and fragile. So, we must take of them.

THEN THE LIFE. **Pictured: a generic single-celled organism looking much like that seen under a microscope in a drop of natural water.** Life is over three billion years old. Life as we know it is cellular, and the first life was single-celled. Many single-celled organisms exist today including fungi, bacteria, algae, and many more. You are made of thirty trillion cells!

FIRST THE GENE. **Pictured: a chromosome and DNA strand with the four nucleotides that come in pairs making the alphabet of genes.** DNA is a very large molecule that holds the instructions for how to build a life-form—like you! Each section of DNA that has a specific instruction—like "grow red hair"—is called a gene. Genes are passed from parents to their offspring and can be inherited.

THEN THE MUTATION. **Pictured: two DNA mutations: a substitution and a deletion.** When DNA is copied, it can be changed. This is called a mutation. Mutations can delete parts of the DNA or replace it. Some mutations do not change genes and some do. Over many generations in a population, this change in genes is called evolution.

FIRST THE FIT. **Pictured: Cooksonia, one of the earliest land plants.** Changes in genes led from single-celled organisms to the variety of plants and animals we see around us. The organisms that are best fit to their environment have the greatest chance to survive and pass on their genes. The first plants were very simple.

THEN THE FITTEST. **Pictured: Montsechia vidalii, the oldest known flowering plant.** Genes can be "selected" by the environment if they led to very successful traits. In environments that do not change much over many generations, unique organisms can arise. These organisms appear as if designed for their environment. Flowering plants now outnumber non-flowering plants nine to one.

FIRST THE TRIBE. **Pictured: handprint cave painting of early humans.** Early humans lived nomadic lives in tribes of few people. This allowed them to migrate great distances and populate the globe. This required the development of tools and methods of communication like language and cave-painting.

THEN THE CIVILIZATION. **Pictured: the Great Sphinx and Pyramids of Giza.** Civilization is thought to have arisen simultaneously in many places around the world several thousand years ago. These quickly developed into dynasties that built statues to honor their rulers and gods.

FIRST THE LOVE. **Pictured: a pair of humans courting.** Genetic and cultural evolution seems to favor monogamy, though not universally. As opposed to other animals, human courtship is uniquely described with emotions. Some of the strongest positive emotions experienced by humans are called love.

THEN THE CHILD. **Pictured: a human child with their caregivers.** A typical human birth produces one offspring, though multiple births can happen. In most modern societies, humans are arranged in families, which comprise the child (or children) and one or two partners who care for and raise the child to adolescence.

FIRST THE SCHOOL. **Pictured: a classic school bell.** Organized education of children in a society is a more recent invention in human history. Compulsory education—the requirement to attend school—exists today in most countries and began only a few hundred years ago in Europe. Schools now also train students to acquire advanced skills requiring many hours of study and practice.

THEN THE DEGREE. **Pictured: an academic cap and diploma.** An academic degree is an award for finishing education beyond the compulsory level. Academic degrees are earned at universities and colleges. The proof of earning a degree is a certificate called a diploma. These are awarded at graduation ceremonies where the students must dress in customary clothing, like square hats with tassels.

FIRST THE PRACTICE. Pictured: a typical set of exercises to practice addition. To become an expert at an advanced skill requires memorization and practice. Whether it is playing the violin, performing surgery, or solving math problems, the more time you spend doing it, the better you will become. A rough guide is the "10,000-Hour Rule," which says you need ten thousand hours of practice to become an expert.

THEN THE EXPERTISE. Pictured: textbooks of all the topics needed to study quarks and the physics of the universe. Expertise is knowledge and skill. Knowledge and skill come from both individual study and guidance from teachers. Each person has unique expertise, so we must all work together to achieve great things.

FIRST THE SCIENTIST. Pictured: Albert Einstein. Albert Einstein is one of the most recognizable scientists in history. He came to fame later in his life after many of his predictions were confirmed in spectacular experiments. Einstein developed many theories and pioneered both branches of modern physics: relativity and quantum physics.

THEN THE THEORY. Pictured: the most famous equation in the world, $E = mc^2$ (Energy equals mass times the speed of light squared.) Theories are mathematical models of the world. They are used to describe what we see around us using advanced scientific equipment. Good theories make predictions about what we haven't seen yet. Great theories give us new insights on the nature of our reality. In Einstein's theory, he showed that energy and matter (mass) are the same thing.

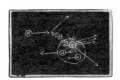

FIRST THE HYPOTHESIS. Pictured: a "Feynman diagram" predicting the interaction of some elementary particles. A hypothesis is a specific prediction about what will happen in an ideal or controlled experiment. Before many elementary particles were observed, their existence was hypothesized using predictions from theories of physics.

THEN THE EXPERIMENT. Pictured: a schematic plan of a linear particle accelerator. Sometimes the details of the experiment are not known and must be designed in order to test hypotheses. This was the case in high-energy physics, where giant experiments needed to be designed and built in order to smash particles together with enough energy to reveal their internal structure.

FIRST THE EXPERIMENT. Pictured: the inside of the largest particle accelerator in the world, the Large Hadron Collider (LHC) in Geneva, Switzerland. Experiments are the workhorses of science. Experiments can strengthen our existing understanding of nature. They can also point to the direction where new understanding can be found. Particle accelerators can be bigger than entire countries and are the largest science experiments humans have ever created.

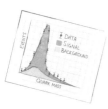

THEN THE DATA. Pictured: a plot summarizing the data from an experiment that measures the mass (or energy) of a quark. The result of an experiment is data. Data is usually quite messy since experiments at the cutting edge of science are difficult to perform. The background, or noise, must not be mistaken for what you are looking for, the signal. Most experiments produce data that is not 100 percent conclusive. There are always margins of error in science.

FIRST THE PARTICLE. Pictured: a proton made of three quarks. We now know protons and neutrons are made of quarks. But this discovery was made possible by science and experimentation. Quarks came before protons, but we needed to smash protons together to discover this fact.

THEN THE QUARK. Pictured: the tracks of elementary particles created when two larger particles are smash together. We cannot see protons with our naked eye, so we definitely cannot see quarks. We can only predict what effect elementary particles have on larger things that we can detect. If the predicted effects are observed in an experiment, we have more confidence that quarks do indeed exist.